Minnie and Moo
Go to Paris

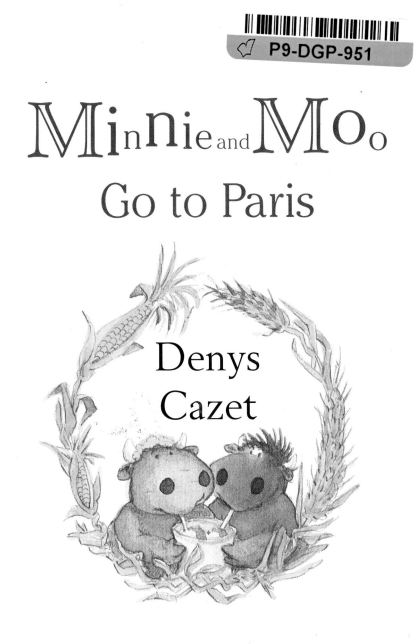

Denys
Cazet

A DK INK BOOK
DK PUBLISHING, INC.

For Frank Rodriguez
mi amigo, mi hermano

A Richard Jackson Book

DK Publishing, Inc., 95 Madison Avenue, New York, New York 10016
Visit us on the World Wide Web at http://www.dk.com
Text and illustrations copyright © 1999 by Denys Cazet

Library of Congress Cataloging-in-Publication Data
Cazet, Denys.
Minnie and Moo go to Paris / by Denys Cazet. — 1st ed.
p. cm.
"A DK Ink book."
Summary: Two cow friends, Minnie and Moo, find a bus
and try to drive to Paris to see the Eiffel Tower.
ISBN 0-7894-2595-5 (hc)   ISBN 0-7894-3928-X (pbk)
[1. Cows—Fiction.   2. Animals—Fiction.   3. Buses—Fiction.   4. Humorous stories.]
I. Title   PZ7.C2985M1 1999   [E]—dc21   98-47421   CIP   AC

The illustrations for this book were created with pencil and watercolor.
The illustration on these pages was drawn in pencil.
The text of this book is set in 18 point Berling.
Printed and bound in U.S.A.
First edition, 1999
(hc)   10 9 8 7 6 5 4 3 2
(pbk) 10 9 8 7 6 5 4 3

Magazines

One spring morning,

Minnie and Moo sat on the hill.

Moo looked at an old magazine.

Minnie chewed on a straw.

"OOOOH," Moo moaned.

"To be in Paris in the spring!"

Minnie looked at the magazine.

"That is a picture of an oil well.

It is in the middle of a street."

"That is *not* an oil well," said Moo.

"That is the Eiffel Tower,

in Paris, France!"

Minnie folded her arms.

"Moo . . . you have been thinking!

It's those magazines!"

"Minnie, it's spring!" said Moo.

"Time for new faces, new places . . .

Paris! Africa! China!"

Minnie sighed.

"Don't you see," said Moo.

"A rolling cow gathers no moss."

Minnie rubbed her bottom.

There was no moss.

"Moo . . . what are you talking about?"

"Seeing the world!" said Moo.

"Moo," said Minnie. "You know
I have to be at the milkers by five."

"I know," said Moo gently.

"If we have to . . . we can skip China."

The Paris Bus

Minnie and Moo sat at the bus stop.

Minnie took a rock out of her shoe.

Moo fixed her shorts.

"Here comes the bus," said Moo.

The bus stopped.

The driver turned the motor off.

Everyone got off the bus.

They crossed the road

and went to lunch.

"What happened?" asked Minnie.

Moo looked across the road.

She looked at the bus.

"I am thinking," said Moo,

"they are done with this bus."

"But Moo . . ."

"Think!" said Moo, tapping her head.

"Use your brain.

When people want to go somewhere,

they get ON the bus.

When people get there,

they get OFF the bus."

"But, Moo. How are we . . ."

"Minnie," said Moo. "Read the sign."

Minnie looked at the side of the bus.

The sign said:

GOT A PLACE TO GO?

TAKE THIS BUS

"We have a place to go," said Moo.

"We will take this bus.

I will drive."

Africa

The bus roared down the road.

It roared past a sign that said:

AFRICA WORLD

AMUSEMENT PARK

(CLOSED)

"MOO, STOP!" Minnie yelled.

"I SEE AFRICA!"

The bus bounced off the road.

It rolled through a gate and stopped.

Minnie and Moo got off the bus.

"Welcome to Africa World,"

said a water buffalo.

"My name is Nadine."

"Hi," said Moo. "I'm Moo.

This is my friend Minnie."

"We're from America," said Minnie.

"Would you like a tour?"

said Nadine, the water buffalo.

"Please," said Moo.

Minnie and Moo toured Africa.

They took a boat ride down the Nile.

They saw alligators with big teeth.

They saw snapping fish.

Once, the boat got caught
in a whirlpool.
It went around and around
and around and around and around.
It made them dizzy.

Another time
it went over a waterfall.
Moo thought it was fun.
Minnie did not.

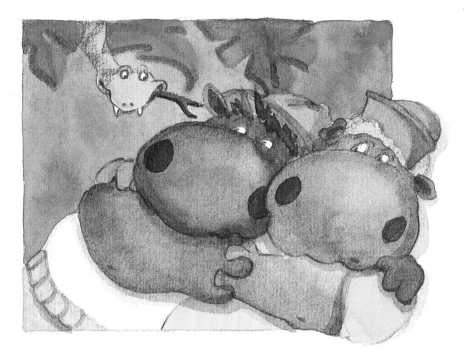

They rode the elephant train

through the deepest, darkest jungle.

Creatures made strange noises.

Something hissed.

Something growled.

Minnie hugged Moo.

Moo hugged Minnie.

They ate lunch in a tree house.

Minnie ordered garden greens,

sweet corn, fava beans,

and two side orders of potato chips.

Moo ordered a bowl of walnuts.

They shared a dessert.

They met many new friends.

"Thank you," said Minnie.

"How can we ever repay you?"

"Take us to America," said Nadine.

Moo smiled.

"All aboard for Paris, China,

and America!"

"Oh, goody!" said Nadine.

"We never go anywhere."

Minnie pointed toward the bus.

"Please get in line," she said.

"Please do not chew gum.

Do not lean out the windows.

And please, for your own safety,

wear your seat belts at all times."

The Eiffel Tower

The bus roared down the road.

It roared past a police car.

Red and blue lights blinked!

"It must be Christmas," said Minnie.

Everyone waved.

"SHORTCUT!" shouted Moo.

The bus flew off the road.

It crossed a muddy field.

It roared through a barn

and up a steep hill.

CLANK!

The bus stopped!

"What happened?" Minnie asked.

"We hit something," said Moo.

Everyone got off the bus.

The bus rested against

an electrical tower.

"MOO!" said Minnie. "LOOK!"

"At last," said Moo softly.

"The Eiffel Tower!"

Minnie looked around.

"Where is Paris?"

"It must be here somewhere," said Moo.

They looked and looked.

"Well, milk me dry!" said Moo.

"Somebody moved it!"

"Where?" said Nadine.

Moo thought.

"China," she said.

China

The bus roared down the hill.

It roared past the police car.

It roared through town.

A sign said:

> CHINA WONG'S

> CAR WASH

"I found China," shouted Minnie.

The bus bounced over the sidewalk.

It bounced into the car wash.

"Does anyone see Paris?" Moo asked.

Everyone looked.

"I can't see anything," said Minnie.

"It is raining too hard!"

"It is a storm," shouted Moo.

"MONSOON," yelled Nadine.

"WITH SOAP SUDS!"

"Close the windows!" yelled Minnie.

The bus shot out of the car wash

and roared down the road.

"There's the farmhouse," said Moo.

Moo slowed the bus down.

She parked the bus in the garage.

At first it wouldn't fit.

But after a few tries

Moo made the garage a little bigger.

"Welcome to America!" said Minnie.

America

They all walked up the hill

to the barn.

"Our tour begins here," said Minnie.

"Minnie!" whispered Moo.

"Here comes the farmer!"

"Oh," gasped Minnie. "I forgot!

My five o'clock milking. . ."

"EVERYONE HIDE!" yelled Moo.

"Hide in the stalls.

Close the doors!"

"Where?" shouted Nadine.

"Stand next to us," said Minnie.

"What about me?" said an ostrich.

"Sit with the chickens," said Moo.

The barn door creaked open.

It was quiet.

The farmer reached for his glasses.

They were gone.

"How am I supposed to milk cows

without glasses?" he muttered.

The farmer slid the milking bucket
under Nadine.

Something was not the same.

Was it this cow?

Was it the strange feet
under the stall doors?

Was it the giant egg
lying on the floor?

40

The barn door squeaked open.

It was the farmer's wife.

"John," she said. "Are you in there?"

"I'm over here," said the farmer.

"Look at the size of this egg!"

"John, there's a policeman here."

"What for?" asked the farmer.

"Something about a bus," she said.

"What bus?"

"The one in our garage!"

Moon Over America

The moon rose.

Someone poked the campfire.

Sparks floated into the night.

After the marshmallows

everyone took turns telling stories.

A monkey told a story

about a talking coconut.

Minnie and Moo told a story

about two cows

who went to the moon.

When the fire died down,

someone sang a sad song

about being far from home.

Minnie, Moo, and Nadine

walked under the stars.

"I'm so lucky," said Nadine.

"All in the same day,

I came to America, met new friends,

and found a nice pair of glasses!"

"New places, new faces," said Moo.

Nadine stopped. "Who lives here?"

"Shhh," said Minnie. "The farmer."

Nadine looked in the window.

The farmer's wife screamed!

The farmer jumped.

"Good gravy, Mildred!

What happened?"

"I found your glasses!" said Mildred.